D1487877

DRAWING ANGELS NEAR

Mimi Doe
and
Garland Waller

POCKET BOOKS

New York   London   Toronto   Sydney   Tokyo   Singapore

POCKET BOOKS, a division of Simon & Schuster Inc.
1230 Avenue of the Americas, New York, NY 10020

ISBN: 0-671-52973-0

First Pocket Books hardcover printing December 1995

10 9 8 7 6 5 4 3 2 1

POCKET and colophon are registered trademarks of
Simon & Schuster Inc.

Printed in Mexico

This collection of angelic wisdom is dedicated to the many children who shared their visions with us. May we all remember and become reacquainted with our own angels.

ACKNOWLEDGMENTS

Mimi: I thank my daughters, Whitney and Lillie, for reintroducing me to the angels, my dear husband, Tom, for his support and love, and my parents for their gift of faith.

Garland: Heartfelt thanks to Alexis, who I believe is Jesse's angel, and to Samantha, who is mine.

FOREWORD

In the beginning our own young children's very vivid accounts of their angels prompted us to talk with other children. We wondered how children of varied backgrounds experienced angels, what they saw, and how they felt about them. We began to collect these stories and incredible pieces of art from children between the ages of 3 and 10. We are thrilled to share them with the world.

Angels came to us through the voices of children. All we did was listen, accept, and record. What we learned was that angels and children have a magical connection. Children don't have to be convinced that angels exist. They know and they see. They enjoy a personal relationship with angels untainted by adult interpretations or traditionalist expectations. Angels speak in words the children understand. As one five-year-old said to us, *"My angel sounds just like me."*

While many adults are looking outside themselves for answers, children are looking inward. As if there were a universal language, children paint their angels and speak of them with a certain reverence and intimacy. They seem to know that they are not alone. From the children we learned that angels are strong, loving friends who are always available. Children operate from a place grownups wish to come back to but have lost in the daily grind of life. Children remind us that angels are an accepted reality that exists for their pure souls. Grownups tend to believe that children's angels are merely by-products of active imaginations. But relegating angels to the world of make-believe does a grave disservice to both child and adult. It denies children their rich inner life, and it denies parents their chance to believe again.

We think one of the reasons children see angels so clearly is that children are angels too. They recognize one another in passing. If we adults would take the time to listen to children's pure voices and acknowledge their inner light, we would see that all children everywhere are gifts to cherish and nurture. If we listen to a child, we may hear the wisdom of the ages. As one seven-year-old said, *"One time a really big angel named Mary took me out flying to meet the really big angel that holds the earth. They made me big too and let me hold the earth for a minute, and it was really heavy."*

Out of the mouths of babes!

My angel helps my sister, and she needs it. (Age 5)

My angel looks like my sister. She is very pretty with a low voice. (Age 6)

Love

I have an angel that helps me, and her twin sister helps my mom. (Age 5)

She likes to walk.
She wants to talk
about everything.
Her likes to play
with little toys. (Age 3)

My angel makes stuff not break.
(Age 3)

When I was a baby I used to cry "waa, waa, waa" until my angel came. (Age 3)

My angel she is always near. On my shoulder she sits, guiding me with every step I take. My angel—oh, I love her so, and I know deep inside she loves me.

(Age 5)

When angels wave their arms, it makes music. (Age 8)

My angel sounds just like me. (Age 5)

She has a high
voice like a
singing star.

(Age 5)

Good night, my little angel.
I hope that you are well,
Because it is time for sleepy bye.
Can't you hear the tinkling bell?

(Age 6)

An angel has wings and lives up in the sky. They talk to children in their hearts. (Age 6)

An angel is something that has wings and looks after you when you're sleeping. I felt it in my bed last night and it kept my legs warm. "Good morning, Elyssa. Did you feel me last night?" Cupid. (Age 6)

An angel is a bird with a person in the middle. (Age 4)

Angels are silent. They just are there for you. It is like an inside thing. (Age 7)

My angel builds up my confidence when I am feeling frustrated and scared. (Age 7)

Under my bed is
my secret place.
That is where I go
to think about
angels and things.

(Age 4)

One time I was in bed and dreamed an angel was sleeping next to me. She had a beautiful black face and black wings and she was pretty. (Age 4)

Angels always walk on their tiptoes.

(Age 6)

Angel of love makes sure you're never alone and always has friends. It tells you to be kind to people. *(age 9)*

Angels love all of the children in the world.

(Age 6)

I love my angel. I feel his love. (Age 4)

My angel has all the powers of the universe in his wings. (Age 9)

My angel looks like a clump of snow on a sunny day. (Age 3)

In my dreams I was flying with the snow angel. (Age 3)

I see light that looks like the light I turn on, and it's all around her. She drops down and warms my tummy. (Age 4)

Angels make their homes
in kitchens. They eat
clouds for food. Kids
become angels if
they are touched
by an angel. (Age 5)

They have wings. Cats can be angels too.

(Age 5)

An angel is a kind of fairy that controls the weather. When it's sunny, they've lit

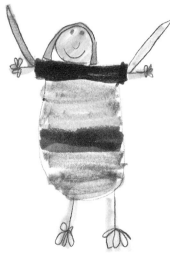

a candle. When it is raining, it is their tears. Thunder is those angels bowling, and when it is snowing, the angels are having a pillow fight. When leaves fall from the trees in the fall, the angel people are coloring paper and fluttering it down. My angel's name is Thumblestorm. (Age 5)

SOPHINA

Sophine is a beautiful angel. "One Who Brings Me Flowers" is her other name. This angel does not go downstairs. She always comes to my room while I am asleep and makes my flowers grow. Her magic water makes my flowers grow and grow and grow. She does a good job, because she makes them pretty and nice. She makes the flowers the colors they are supposed to be. My mom wanted to know more about my angel. Mommy had a sick plant that she was going to throw away. I asked her to put it in my room. The next morning there were four little flowers right in the middle of the plant. I love my angel. Do you love yours? (Age 4)

I used to be an angel. My mommy and daddy say I came from mommy's tummy, but my story is different. (Age 5)

When I was in New Zealand just being born, I saw it—saw an angel named Orange because it was all orange. (Age 4)

I used to be an angel and watched over my mommy when she was a little girl. I picked her to be my mommy. When it was my turn to come down, I asked my angel friend Lanya to take over for me and then I was born. *(Age 5)*

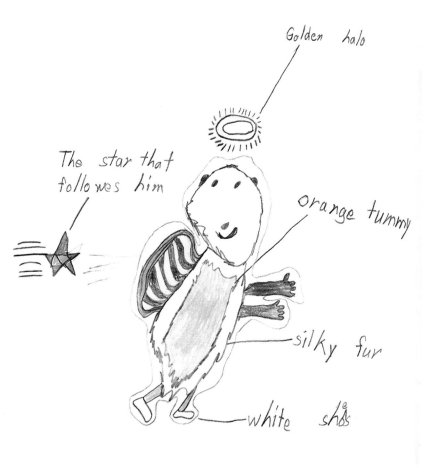

Golden halo

The star that follows him

orange tummy

silky fur

white shoe

A long time ago when I was born, I thought of all the things I had made before. It was that time that I knew the angels. (Age 4)

Before my uncle died of AIDS, he told me that he would always be with me. That he would be an angel watching over me. He said that I would know he was around because I would find a feather from his wings. I've been looking and looking for feathers in the snow. Last night I found one right on my pillow. (Age 7)

An angel with a broken heart
(Age 7)

They could make everybody happy if only people would listen. (Age 4)

ABOUT THE AUTHORS

Mimi Doe holds a Master's Degree in Education from Harvard University. She leads workshops across the country on the inner life of children. Garland Waller is an award-winning television producer listed in *Who's Who of American Women*; her credits include many children's programs for Boston's WBZ-TV, as well as the Lifetime series *Your Child 6–12*. They merged their talents to create the nationally acclaimed special *This Secret Should Be Told*. Co-founders of Pink Bubble Productions, they developed the pilot for a new concept in children's programming, *Angel-Land*.

Mimi Doe and Garland Waller have created a delightful, 25-minute videotape for children ages 2–6, called *Concert in Angel-Land*. To order call: 1-800-777-ANGEL, or send $15.95 + $3.95 for shipping and handling to:

> Pink Bubble Productions
> P.O. Box 157
> Concord, MA 01742